Fun to do
MODELLING

Joan Jones

CONTENTS

FITZGERALD BOOKS

What You Will Need

Before you begin to make your models it is a good idea to get ready a few useful tools. You will need scissors for cutting; a pencil, eraser and ruler for drawing and marking off; glue for fixing things together; and paint and felt-tip pens for decorating. A light coat of varnish will give your models a shiny finish.

Kitchen Equipment

You will also need some standard kitchen tools including:

Measuring jug, mixing bowl, bucket, plastic bowl, measuring spoons, baking tray, greaseproof paper, cling film, chopping board, oven gloves, plastic spatula, wooden spoon, saucepan

Petroleum jelly

Ruler

Pencil and eraser

Felt-tip pens

Poster paints

Brushes

Other Useful Things

To cut and mark dough and clay
Plastic bottle tops, pen tops, jar lids, spoon handles, fork prongs, paper-clips, buttons, children's knitting needles, straws, pasta, thread bobbins, garlic press, cocktail sticks

For plaster molds
Any empty plastic food containers: yogurt cartons, egg trays, chocolate box trays, etc.

To decorate your models
Material scraps, felt, pipe cleaners, glitter, straws, buttons, pasta, beads, seeds, sequins, ribbons, pine cones, dried leaves and flowers, tree bark, shells, pebbles

Hole punch

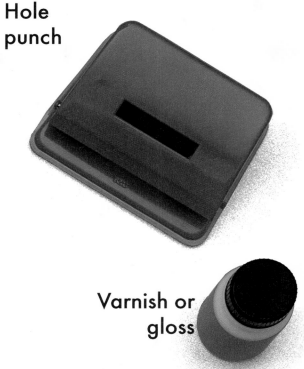

Varnish or gloss

Glue spreader

Child's rolling-pin

White Glue

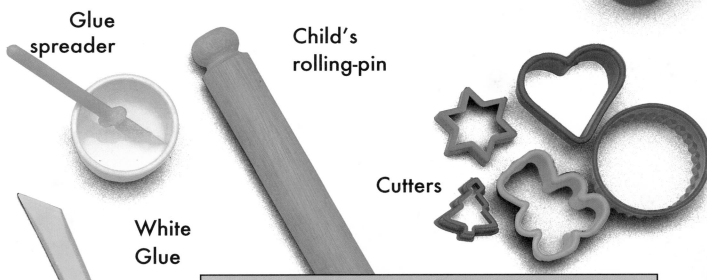

Cutters

Modelling tool

Remember

☆ Wear an apron and cover the work area.
☆ Collect together the items in the materials box at the beginning of each project.
☆ Always ask an adult for help when you see this sign [!]
☆ Clear up after yourself.

Scissors

Play Dough Fun

Play dough is quick and easy to make, but as it involves cooking you will need to ask a grown up to help you.

Materials

food coloring

3 1/2 oz plain white flour

1 teaspoon cream of tartar

1 teaspoon cooking oil

1 3/4 oz salt

4 1/2 fl oz water

1 Put the flour, salt, cream of tartar and cooking oil into a saucepan and stir together.

2 Add 1–2 teaspoonfuls of red food coloring to the water and stir well. The more you add the deeper the color will be.

3 Gradually add the water to the other ingredients, mixing thoroughly to remove any lumps.

[!] 4 Cook over a low to medium heat. Stir continuously until the dough becomes thick and leaves the sides of the pan almost clean.

⚠ 5 Scrape the mixture from the saucepan onto a smooth flat surface. Put the saucepan into soak immediately. Make up two more batches of blue and yellow play dough.

⚠ 6 Leave the play dough to cool for at least ten minutes. Before using the dough ask an adult to cut through it with a knife to test that the inside has cooled too.

7 Knead the cooled play dough until it becomes smooth and pliable. You can mix the three colors to get a marbled effect.

8 You can make up a variety of colors by mixing together red, yellow and blue.
Red and yellow makes orange.
Blue and yellow makes green.
Red and blue makes purple.

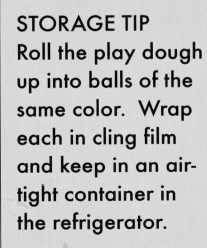

STORAGE TIP
Roll the play dough up into balls of the same color. Wrap each in cling film and keep in an airtight container in the refrigerator.

Play Dough Pictures

Roll out a ball of all the different colored play dough you have made.

Materials

colored card

colored play dough

pipe cleaners

sequins

buttons

1 Cut out rectangles and squares from the rolled out play dough. Cut the squares in half to make triangles, and cut the triangles in half to make even smaller triangles.

2 Use bottle tops, jar lids and pastry cutters to cut out circles, ovals and crescent shapes.

3 Now start to put these shapes together onto backgrounds of colored card to make pictures.

4 You can add detail to your pictures in all sorts of ways. A cotton reel pressed into a play dough circle makes great tractor wheels.

5 Use a cocktail stick to mark 'fur' onto a play dough animal.

6 A button bow tie and pipe cleaner whiskers finish off this cat *purr*fectly.

7 A paper-clip can be used to mark on bird feathers or fish scales.

You can have lots of fun putting the finishing touches to your picture.

Play Dough Bakery

Remember, although these things look good enough to eat they wouldn't taste nice at all, so please don't try it!

Iced cherry cakes

1 Roll some small and large balls of the red play dough and some medium-sized balls of the yellow play dough.

Croissants

3 Roll out some yellow play dough until it is very thin. Cut into squares.

Materials

colored play dough

plate

baking cups

2 Flatten a yellow ball between your fingers and drape over a large red ball. Top with a small red ball.

4 Roll up a square from one corner. Bend into a crescent shape.

Jam tarts

5 Roll out some yellow play dough to about ¼in thick and cut out some circles with a small pastry cutter.

6 Press a small bottle top in the center of each cut circle to make an indentation.

7 Place a ball of red or yellow play dough in the hollow and flatten to fill the space.

Why not try modelling a variety of fruits from your play dough, such as oranges, apples, cherries, grapes, bananas and pears. Use pipe cleaners to make stalks and leaves.

Salt Dough Medallions

Salt dough can be baked hard, painted and varnished so that you can keep the things you make forever.

Materials

ribbon

gold card

1 teaspoon cooking oil

$2\frac{1}{2}$ fl oz water

$3\frac{1}{2}$ oz plain white flour

$1\frac{3}{4}$ oz salt

1 Mix together the salt, flour and cooking oil in a bowl. Add the water a little at a time and mix to a smooth paste that leaves the sides of the bowl clean.

2 Place the dough onto a lightly-floured board. Use a lightly-floured rolling-pin to roll out the dough to about $\frac{1}{4}$ in thick.

3 Use pastry cutters to cut out several shapes from the salt dough.

4 Use a paper-clip to print a pattern on the medallions.

10

! **5** Open out the paper-clip and prick out a circular pattern on the medallions. Place them onto a greased baking tray and bake in a pre-heated oven at 250°F until they are firm (about 2 hours).

! **6** Remove the medallions from the oven and leave to cool. Paint and lightly varnish. Decorate the medallions. To make a winning medal, cut a star from gold card and glue onto the center of one of the medallions.

7 Overlap the ends of the ribbon and glue together. Stick the medallion firmly to the overlapped ends of the ribbon.

The medallions can easily be changed into badges by simply taping a safety pin to the back of the decorated shapes.

Materials

ribbon

salt dough

felt

two pipe cleaners

material

Faces on the Door

Follow the instructions for making salt dough on page 10, then use it to model these jolly faces to hang over your bedroom door.

1 Lightly flour your hands and a board. Knead the dough on the board until it is smooth. Break off a small piece and put to one side.

2 Press the larger ball of dough into a face shape about ½in thick. To make the eyes and mouth twist a pencil into the face.

3 Break the remaining dough into two and shape a nose and a moustache. Use a little water to lightly wet the back of each piece and position onto the face.

⚠ 4 Bake in a pre-heated oven on a greased baking tray at 250°F for 3-4 hours until firm. When cool, paint and varnish.

5 Cut an eye patch and band from the felt. Position on the face and secure with glue at the back of the head.

6 Make an earring by twisting a pipe cleaner into a circle. Glue to the side of the pirate's head.

7 Wrap the material around the pirate's head and secure on one side with the other pipe cleaner. Glue the finished head onto a long piece of ribbon.

Hang the completed faces over your cupboard or bedroom doors. You could model smaller faces and hang these from drawers.

A Christmas Decoration

To color the salt dough, simply follow the recipe on page 10, but add 1 tablespoon of red food coloring to the mixing water.

Materials

glitter

red salt dough

wide red ribbon

narrow red ribbon

tinsel

2 baubles

florists' fine gauge wire

2 sprigs holly

1 On a lightly-floured board, roll the salt dough into a thick sausage shape about 12in long. Make a hole with a pencil at one end of the sausage and model the other end into a point.

! **2** Place onto a greased baking tray and form into a circle. Moisten the pointed end and put into the hole. Smooth the join. Score the top of the ring with a plastic knife. Bake in a pre-heated oven for 3-4 hours at 250°F until firm, turning occasionally. Set aside to cool.

3 Lightly spread glue across the top of the dough circle and sprinkle on the glitter. Stick tinsel around the edge.

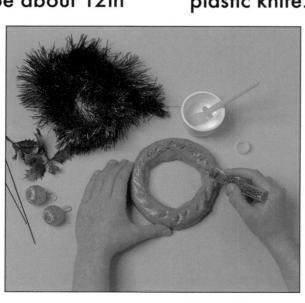

4 Thread the baubles onto the florists' wire. Twist the wire to keep them in place. Position the baubles on the bottom edge of the circle and secure by firmly winding the wire around the dough circle.

5 To hide the wire, wrap the wide ribbon between the baubles and tie into a bow. Glue the ends of the holly sprigs and tuck into the bow.

6 Thread the narrow ribbon through the top of the circle and knot to make a loop for hanging up the decoration. Tie the ribbon ends into a bow.

Pots of Fun

The models on the next few pages have been made using air-hardening clay. This will need to be left for a few days in a cool, dry place. But the end results will be well worth the wait!

1 Take 2 small lumps of clay and shape into balls between the palms of your hands.

2 Flatten the balls with your fingers.

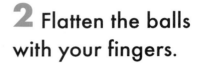
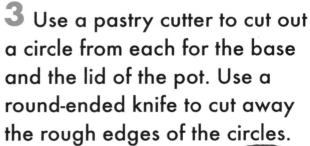

3 Use a pastry cutter to cut out a circle from each for the base and the lid of the pot. Use a round-ended knife to cut away the rough edges of the circles.

4 Roll out a sausage approximately $1/4$in thick and long enough to fit around the inside edge of one of the circles. Roll another 4 sausages of the same length and thickness.

5 Trim each end of the sausages with a diagonal cut. Now wet and gently press together the ends of each sausage to make a perfect coil.

6 Place a coil on the inside edge of one of the circles. Build up the pot by wetting and placing the remaining coils on top of each other.

You can have lots of fun decorating the pots and the lids.

STORAGE TIP
Once opened you can stop the clay drying out by wrapping it in foil or cling film and storing it in a plastic bag.

7 To make the pot lid, roll a small ball of clay and place in the center of the second circle. Leave the pot and lid to harden in a cool, dry place for several days. Paint and varnish.

A Woodland Scene

This collection of clay animals will bring a touch of nature to your bedroom. If you run out of clay, you could use salt dough instead.

The spider

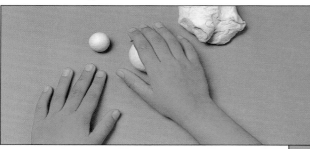

Materials

pine cones, leaves and tree bark

air-hardening clay

felt

glitter

spent matchstick

pipe cleaners

1 Roll out 2 balls of clay, a large one for the body and a small one for the head.

2 Push the spent matchstick into the body, leaving about $1/2$in sticking out. Push on the head.

3 Use a cocktail stick to mark hairs over the body and the head.

The ladybird

4 Take a small ball of clay and model it into a ladybird shape. Use a cocktail stick to mark in the head and the wings.

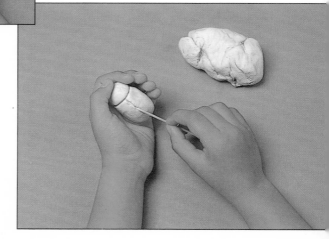

The snail

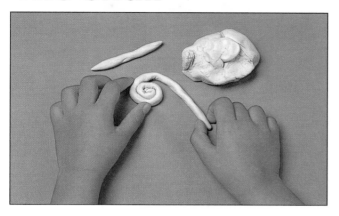

5 Roll a long and a short sausage from the clay. Roll up the long sausage into a coil and place on the shorter sausage.

6 Use a cocktail stick to mark in the snail's eyes and mouth, and to decorate the shell.

7 Leave the clay animals to dry out for several days, then paint and varnish them. Glue 8 pipe cleaner legs to the underside of the spider and 6 to the ladybird. Stick 8 black felt spots to the ladybird's back. Glue glitter on the spider's head.

Make a woodland scene on green card to display your clay animals. Decorate with stones, pine cones, leaves, dried flowers and tree bark

19

Lighthouse Picture

Make this super picture for your bedroom wall. You can use salt dough instead of clay if you prefer.

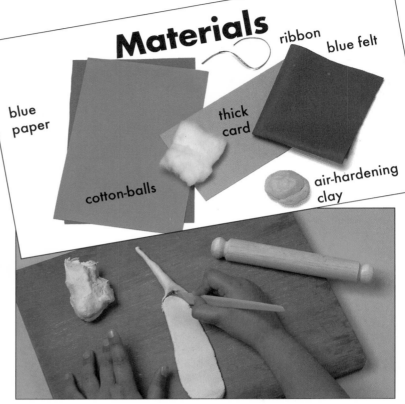

Materials

blue paper

cotton-balls

thick card

ribbon

blue felt

air-hardening clay

1 Roll some clay into a long sausage, thicker at one end than the other. Flatten using a rolling-pin.

2 Use a round-ended knife or modelling tool to cut out a lighthouse shape from the flattened clay.

3 Mark in the lantern house, windows and doors.

4 Shape the leftover clay into jagged rocks. Lay all the clay pieces onto a cling film-covered board and leave to harden for several days in a cool, dry place.

20

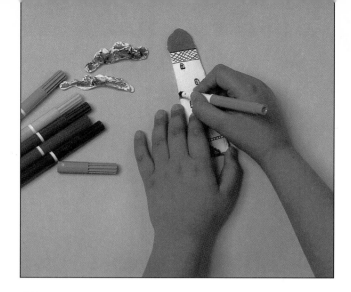

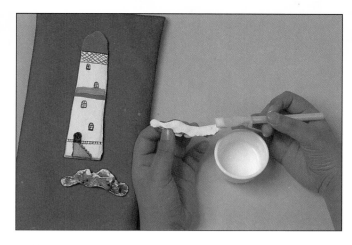

5 Paint the rocks brown and the lighthouse white. Once the paint has dried, use felt-tip pens to mark in details on the lighthouse.

6 Cut a piece of card 11in x 5½in and cover with the felt. Stick the lighthouse in the center of the card. Position the rocks beneath the lighthouse and glue in place.

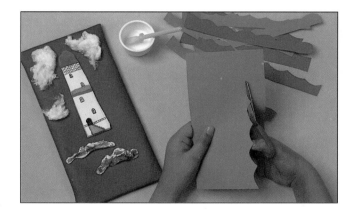

7 Cut wave shapes from blue paper and glue in place beneath the lighthouse and around the rocks. Stick cotton-ball clouds in the sky.

8 Punch 2 holes at the top of the card and thread a ribbon through for hanging up the picture.

21

Cone People

Papier mâché simply means 'mashed paper'. You can model it into any shape with your hands or by applying it to a mold. But it is a messy business and rubber gloves may be a good idea.

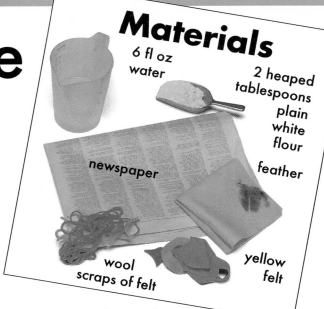

Materials

6 fl oz water

2 heaped tablespoons plain white flour

newspaper

feather

wool scraps of felt

yellow felt

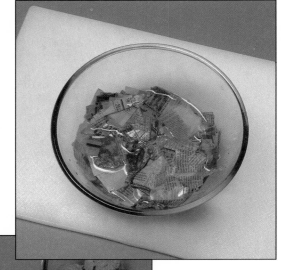

1 Tear the newspaper into lengths about 1 in wide. Tear these strips again into small pieces about 1 in square. Put into a container.

! **2** Cover the torn paper with hot water and leave to soak overnight.

3 Take handfuls of paper and squeeze the water out. Place the squeezed-out paper into another bowl. Empty the water from the container.

4 Put the flour in the mixing jug. Add the water slowly and mix to a smooth, creamy paste.

5 Put the squeezed paper back into the bucket a little at a time, mixing it with small amounts of paste until it becomes a smooth pulp. You may need to mix more paste.

6 Take a handful of papier mâché and work into a cone. Smooth the sides. Leave to dry in a warm, dry place for several days.

7 Paint the cone with 2 coats of bright paint. When dry, paint on the eyes, nose and mouth.

8 Glue some short strands of wool around the sides and back of the head, about 1½in from the top of the cone. Cut out a felt hoop large enough to fit over the top of the cone just above the hair. Add a feather.

If you cannot make a cone shape, make one that is rounded at the top instead, just like the little red model on the end.

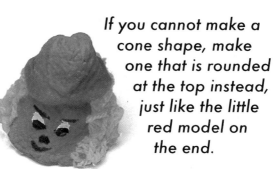

Papier Mâché Boat

A *plastic bottle cut in half makes a perfect mold for making the hull of a boat from mashed paper.*

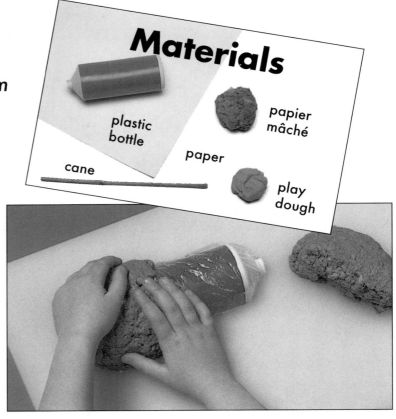

Materials

plastic bottle

papier mâché

paper

cane

play dough

1 Cut a small plastic bottle in half lengthways. Cover one half with cling film.

2 Spread papier mâché evenly over the half bottle mold until it is about $1/4$in thick. Leave to dry in a warm, dry place for several days.

3 Carefully ease the bottle and cling film from the papier mâché. Leave for a further day or two to let the inside dry out thoroughly.

4 Paint the boat inside and out. Several coats of paint may be needed. Once the paint has dried, the hull can be varnished.

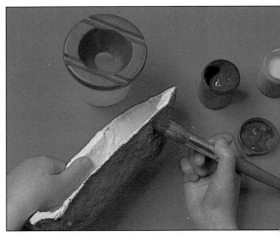

5 To make a sail, cut a piece of paper 9½in x 8in and decorate with felt-tip pens.

6 Punch a hole at the center top and center bottom of the sail. Slip the sail onto the cane.

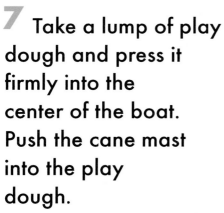

7 Take a lump of play dough and press it firmly into the center of the boat. Push the cane mast into the play dough.

To make your boat into a Viking ship, cut out and decorate some circles for shields. Stick them along each side of the boat.

Papier Mâché Plate

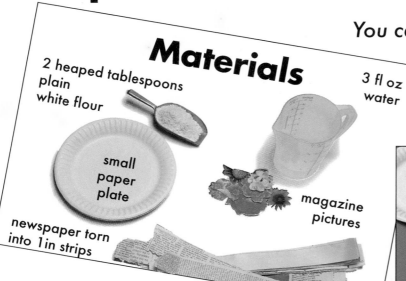

Materials

2 heaped tablespoons plain white flour

small paper plate

newspaper torn into 1 in strips

3 fl oz water

magazine pictures

You can make this beautiful plate from just a few old newspapers and magazines.

1 Place the flour into a mixing jug. Gradually add the water to it to mix to a smooth, slightly runny paste.

2 Cover the front of the plate with petroleum jelly. Put a layer of newspaper strips on top. Paste well, smoothing down the paper with your fingers.

3 Lay a second layer of newspaper strips over the first layer, but in the opposite direction. Continue pasting and adding layers of newspaper strips first in one direction, then the other, until 8 layers have been completed.

4 Leave to harden for several days in a cool, dry place. When completely dry, remove the papier mâché carefully from the plate. Trim the edge with scissors to neaten.

To make this sun mobile, cut the edges of the papier mâché plate into sun ray shapes. Add a circle of beads and buttons to the center and glue firmly in place. Spray the front and back with gold paint.

5 Paint the back of the plate. You may need several coats to cover the newspaper.

6 Decorate the front of the plate by gluing on magazine pictures.

7 Paint a light varnish over the finished plate.

Plaster Eggs

Modelling plaster or plaster of Paris as it is often known is used to make these decorative eggs.

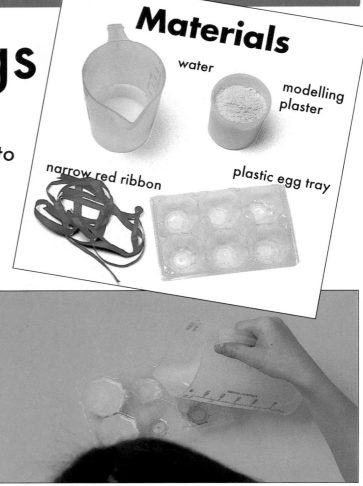

Materials

water

modelling plaster

narrow red ribbon

plastic egg tray

1 Wipe the inside of the egg tray with dishwashing liquid.

2 Mix 2 cups of plaster to 1 cup of water. Pour the liquid plaster into the egg tray. Allow to dry and harden for about an hour.

3 Remove the half egg shapes from the tray and paint. Glue two painted halves together.

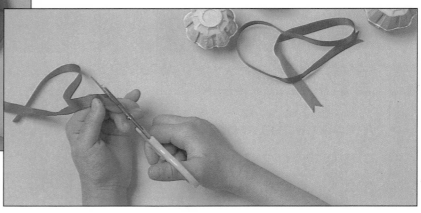

4 Cut the ribbon into 6, 21in lengths and 3, 10in lengths.

28

5 Wrap a long piece of ribbon around the egg and tie in a knot at the top.

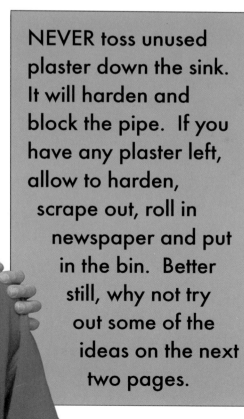

6 Tie a second long piece of ribbon around the egg and secure with a knot. Knot the ends of both ribbons together so that the egg can be hung up.

7 Take a short piece of ribbon and tie into a decorative bow at the top of the egg.

NEVER toss unused plaster down the sink. It will harden and block the pipe. If you have any plaster left, allow to harden, scrape out, roll in newspaper and put in the bin. Better still, why not try out some of the ideas on the next two pages.

Materials

modelling plaster

play dough

cocktail sticks

felt

dried flowers

thin white card

yogurt carton

egg tray

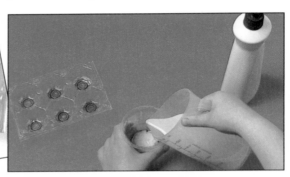

Odds and Ends

Think twice before throwing away any plastic packaging from food products. All make excellent molds for plaster casting. Here are some simple ideas for you to try out.

1 Wipe the insides of the plastic molds with dishwashing liquid, and fill with modelling plaster. Leave to harden, then carefully remove from the molds.

Windmill

2 Paint the yogurt cast white and an egg cast red. When this has dried, paint in doors and windows on the yogurt cast. Glue the egg cast to the top of the yogurt cast.

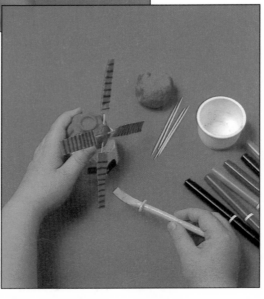

3 Cut out 4 sails from white card and decorate. Glue to the cocktail sticks and attach to the front of the windmill with play dough.

Party Place Names

4 Paint the remaining 5 egg casts in bright colors and leave to dry. Glue felt leaves and a dried flower to the top of each.

5 Write the names of your friends or family onto small rectangles of white card and stick to the bottom of each decorated cast.

Handprint Paperweight

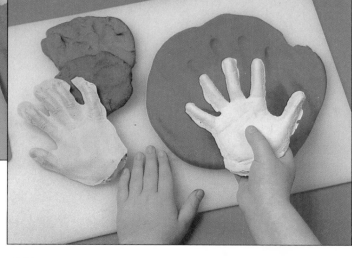

6 Roll out a large ball of play dough to about ¹/₂in thick. Firmly press your hand into the play dough. Fold up the bottom edge of the play dough if it has become flattened out. Fill the mold with plaster and leave to dry for several hours.

7 Carefully peel away the play dough from the plaster cast. Paint and varnish. Use the plaster hand to keep your drawings in place and store paper-clips in the palm.

Advice to Grown Ups

Tools and Materials

Paint Poster or acrylic paints are suitable for painting all the models in this book. From a small selection of paints, red, yellow, black and white, all other colors can be obtained by mixing. Encourage your child to explore color mixing for themselves. Always ensure that paint has dried before applying varnish or decorations.

Felt-tip pens A good set of felt-tip pens is essential for adding fine detail to models.

Glue White glue is recommended as it is versatile, clean, strong and safe.

Varnish Varnishing is optional but a light coat of clear varnish will protect the finished models. Buy non-toxic varnish that is suitable for children to use, available from most art and craft shops. Alternatively watered-down white glue can be used. Always ensure that the varnish has completely dried before adding any decorations.

Scissors For safety's sake children should use small scissors with round-ended metal blades and plastic handles. These will not cut thick card or material easily and this is best done by an adult.

Modelling tools A child-size rolling-pin is advisable for rolling out play dough, salt dough and clay prior to cutting. For cutting, children can use a round-ended knife or modelling tool, bottle tops, jar lids and pastry cutters. Care should be taken with metal pastry cutters: if accidentally placed the wrong way up and pressed hard, they could cut the hand.

Play Dough

Play dough can be bought readymade. It is also incredibly simple to make and a recipe has been given in this book. Play dough that has been stored in the refrigerator may require a few drops of oil to be kneaded into it to make it pliable.

Salt Dough

Salt dough can be baked in an oven, decorated and varnished, so that models made with it can be kept forever. In the recipe given on page 10 only a rough guide to the amount of water needed is provided. It is important to add the water *a little at a time*, until the salt dough leaves the bowl and hands clean. Salt dough is best made the day before it is required. Store in a plastic bag in the refrigerator. Before using knead well on a lightly-floured board.

When joining large areas of salt dough (and clay), lightly scratch the surface with a knife first. For smaller areas, lightly moisten with water and join two pieces together smoothing them carefully to hide the join.

Before baking modelled articles, brush lightly with a little water to give a good finish. Place items on a lightly-greased baking tray. Salt dough should be cooked slowly in the oven on a low heat (250°F). Small articles will take about 1–2 hours, larger models will need 3–4 hours. Better still, cook overnight on the lowest setting. If possible turn the salt dough models over halfway through baking to ensure that they are cooked through.

NOTE: Salt dough cannot be cooked in a microwave oven.

Air-hardening Clay

Clay does not need a kiln to harden it; it will dry hard in a few days if left in a cool, dry place. It can be bought from art and craft shops. Once opened, the clay will keep if wrapped in foil or cling film and placed in a plastic bag.

Papier Mâché

There are two methods for making papier mâché:

The Layered Method Lay strips of torn newspaper over a mold and paste each layer with flour paste. To make paste: approx. 2 heaped tablespoons plain white flour io 3 fl oz water.

The Pulp Method Tear newspaper into small squares and mix with a flour paste to make a malleable pulp. To make paste: approx. 2 heaped tablespoons plain white flour to 6 fl oz water. Making pulp papier mâché is a messy business: use old but clean containers and wear rubber gloves.

Before decorating, papier mâché models must be left for several days to dry out completely in a dry, moderately warm place, otherwise fungus will form.

Modelling Plaster

Modelling plaster (plaster of Paris) can be purchased from most art and craft shops. It is normally mixed at 2 portions of plaster to 1 of water, but this may vary slightly. Plastic packaging from food products make excellent molds. Wipe the mold with neat dishwashing liquid so that it will release the plaster cast easily once it has set. If the mold will not come away, it can be cut with scissors and carefully stripped.

Library of Congress Cataloging-in-Publication Data

Jones, Joan.
    Modelling / Joan Jones — 1st Americanized ed.
        p. cm. — (Fun to do)
    Summary: Explains how to make models and games using salt materials such as play dough, papier-mache, and salt dough.
    ISBN 1-887238-03-4
    1. Models and modeling—Juvenile literature.
    2. Modeling—Juvenile literature. [1. Modeling.
    2. Handicraft.] I. Title. II. Series.
TT916.J65   1995
731.4'2—dc20   95-060780

Fitzgerald Books
100 North 16th Street
Bethany, MO 64424

Project Editor: Cheryl Brown
Primary Designer: Anita Ruddell
Additional Design: Shari Tikus, Karen Knutson
Photography: Jon Bochier
Filmwork: Scantrans Pte Limited

The publisher would like to thank the children and staff of the Early Learning Center, and the Riversdale Primary School, London, Borough of Wandsworth, for their help in producing these books.